Sight

Breanna McNamara

BookLeaf
Publishing

Presentation by *BookLeaf Publishing*

Web: www.bookleafpub.com

E-mail: info@bookleafpub.com

ISBN: 9789357214155

First edition 2023

To my mom and dad who have encouraged every dream, I've ever had.

To my friends and family who have been supportive of every choice, I've ever made and remained in my corner even on my darkest days.

To my students who inspire me every day to keep my passions alive and to always do my best.

To the man who set a fire in me that won't ever die.

ACKNOWLEDGEMENT

My world is full of color because of the souls who have touched it. I'm appreciative of every shade that has ever been swirled into my abyss for it has made me the mosaic masterpiece that I am. I would have nothing to write about if it weren't for those I have experienced and for those who have experienced me.

PREFACE

Often times I'm overwhelmed by my existence and what it means to be human. The way I am able to feel things so intensely-- I'm convinced emotions/feelings/words will always be more painful than any physical pain I could experience. There are times when I'm unable to make sense of my feelings, so I put them into words to the best of my abilities. They don't always translate, but they always make sense to me. The whole reason I write is to know and understand myself better and hope that my words are able to help someone else make sense of a feeling they can't put a name to.

Pages of Partners

Believe me when I say that if I've ever loved
you, or if you've ever hurt me–
your name will be blurred somewhere between
the lines I write and the pages they rest on.
Take it as a compliment that you have affected
me in a way worth writing about.

I can still feel all my lovers within the pages of
my chapters,
each one holding a fleeting feeling or lesson
learned.
Some, long past, and some tend to resurface at
just the right time.
The fold in the corner of the page holds the spot
where we left off.

I harbor many books with folded pages–
thinking it was a story I would come back to, but
never did.
I hope they found a better place than the shelf
and did something with the dust that settled
there.

I take their lust as it comes. No lover ever the
same as the other and yet,

I find things in all of them that I appreciate.
Some I've even grown to love.
These experiences cannot be duplicated, much
like the individuals who helped create them.

I wonder if I'm ever thought of this in this way–
am I the fairy tale waiting to be uncovered?
Am I the story that gets folded at the corner,
paused on a particular page
with the intention of coming back, or have I
become an archived volume,
put into the restricted section in hopes someone
will be daring enough to seek me out?

What am I to your story, but a page folded at the
corner, never to be returned to again?

Haiku #1

Fell in love with you,
but not in the way I thought;
an illusion lost.

My Therapist Doesn't Even Get It

"When something you deem bad occurs,
you revert back to your old ways
and relive your trauma."

Once you've experienced gold,
plated silver won't do.

Don't expect you to understand
what you've never had.

It's easy to assume
that it was less than perfect,
but you weren't there.

You have no idea
of the feelings experienced–
the love shared.

If you did, you'd understand
why letting go seems so unattainable.

And why settling will never be an option.

"What use is there in the better way of doing
things
when no one else is held accountable for their
part
in bringing me back into this headspace?"

Haiku #2

When you feel alone,
remember the crescent moon.
She shines with no one.

Someone's Choice

You tell yourself that no one will love you
because it's easier than admitting someone just
might.

It's easier to believe that you need no one until
the weight of reality slaps you in the face
and you realize you can't carry this weight
alone,
or maybe you just don't want to.

It's much easier to believe that you're broken
rather than whole
because you're ashamed of the things you've
done
and realize there is fault in your cracks.

It's easier to guard your heart and not allow
anyone in
because you assume they couldn't possibly
understand you.

It's easier to run far away from the truth
rather than to face the fears you have
of allowing someone else to love you.

Someday someone will come along
and love you the way you deserve to be loved,
and perhaps that terrifies you most of all.
Because you won't be able to dismiss it.
You won't be able to manipulate yourself
into believing you aren't deserving of it.

The undeniable free will of another's love.

Reverse Hibernation

Decided to sit this winter out,
ignore the cold and soak in the rays
for as long as the days allow.
A new season might bring its luck;
four leaf clovers are hidden in March to find.
Thirty-two may be the year worth dreaming
again–
I'll let you know by another quarter past.
You tell me if I've changed
or if I'm still the same girl
you have always remembered,
The one that set your dreams on fire,
but became engulfed in the smoke.
Hindsight is twenty-twenty,
but you already knew I'd make it out alive.

Don't Be Tardy

I wasn't ready like I thought I was.
It isn't as simple as it used to be…
before feelings became involved.
I've had to learn to maneuver them in such a
way
that it appears I don't have any at all.
Masking, framing, shaping–
until they are morphed into sentiments of
someone else's creation.

Good representation on a chance meeting
could give someone the wrong impression.

IDGTF

What would people do without their deception?
Actually have to work through their shit and be
real for a change.
Call me an old soul, but is it too much to ask for
common decency,
or has the term become so foreign that humans
can't make meaning of it anymore?
That the words we speak should fulfill what is
being stated,
or are we just hanging on the hope of letters tied
together with empty promises?
I suppose it's easy when there are devices to hide
behind.
I can't bear the thought of every new encounter I
expose myself to
is nothing but a sphere that encompasses an
arrow that points nowhere.
A waste of time, energy, and space to my
precious existence.
I don't have a place for it, nor do I feel anyone
has a space for me
that isn't perfectly positioned at surface level.
I'd rather be displaced.

Pandemic

I was told to put my feelings into words,
so here I am,
trying to make sense of a situation
that has caused me more angst
than I know what to do with.

It was the year I didn't feel alive in my own life.
It was more than the distance that couldn't be
traveled.
It was more than the sharing with family and
friends that couldn't be had.
It was more than the separation I felt between
my lover and me.
It was more than "writer's block."
It was more than the feeling that "this too shall
pass."

Days turned into weeks,
weeks into months–
the habitual nature of holding on to the hope
that tomorrow will bring a new notion,
but things are just as they are…
not the same.

Possibilities used to be endless.

The dreams I dreamt of used to be infinite.
Now I feel stuck in neutral.
Not moving backward (never),
but not moving forward (either).
My life changed in some permanent way,
but the effects have yet to be determined.

S.C.

Standing tall like a tree,
your roots embedded in the good times.
Limbs wrapped in laughter and sincerity;
branches filled with leaves of charisma–
intrigued by how their colors will change.

You've helped me view things differently
beneath the shade tree.
And who knew my perception needed to be
shifted
from dark bark to evergreen?
A veiled canopy of emerald penetrating
ever-changing light;
your branch is a hand and it feels like a friend.

Light-hearted and carefree,
you make being around you feel like a breeze.
Plant yourself in the notion that you are a
natural;
a true rarity at its finest.
Much like a tree–
you bring peace.

Haiku #3

Like the four seasons,
we change colors many times.
We are we no more.

B.B

I believe there is good in the world
because you exist–
a bright spot that captures every eye.
And you don't even know
of the light you shone.
Even in your darkest hour–
no one quite compares to you.

I believe in soul mates
because you exist–
never have I ever had someone
know my heart the way you do.
Every dark thought,
every cruel intention,
every senseless notion.
And you've loved me just the same.
Even after everything this life has put us
through–
you are the constant.

I believe in the certainties of the universe
because you exist–
consistent, loyal, and true.
You rise like the morning sun
and fall into the phases of the moon.

You're a star I look up to
when I'm unsure of where to go,
you always guide me home.

A Death in Springtime

The season brought its warmth
and with it, the numbered days.
I knew you would be taken from me
in a matter of hours, so I couldn't stay away.

I looked straight into your eyes
and relived every memory we ever made,
however short-lived.

The same black and white dress;
fingers perfectly entwined.
Time and blood morphed your body,
but your heart remained the same.

I felt shame that night I made you cry.
My selfishness, even for a moment,
meant that I was hurting you
because I couldn't understand
what you already knew.

Life would go on,
but nothing would ever be the same as it was,
and in that, you found a blessing.
One that I'm still not sure I see.

You saw a light in me
I was unable to see in myself,
and perhaps it has dimmed
now that you went away.

I'm not the same.
Perhaps even worse off than I was
before I ever knew you existed,
but how can that be?
I feel this way because
nothing has quite compared since,
and how is that fair?
That this feeling that I crave
can only be fulfilled by you
and you aren't here.

I'm happy, sad, and angry
all at the same time,
and that's if I'm putting it lightly.

I'm happy that I knew you.
I'm sad that it didn't last.
I'm angry that you no longer get to live.

But I know love abides, even in death.
So I'll stay perfectly positioned until the time
comes.

The array of feelings that cast inside of me

could blow this place to pieces,
but who would be left beneath the rubble?

M.

Desire never held any meaning
until I knew of you.
The only words that ever meant anything
were the ones you wrote,
about your hands upon my skin.

They are still the only ones that matter now–
At least in terms of you.

Can't seem to make sense of the way
you easily disconnect without a trace;
and yet, you leave me lusting for more
of whatever it is you have
that the others don't.

I'll tuck away some blank pages,
perhaps to be used on a rainy day–
they'll be filled with lines of a decent fuck,
but first I'd have to give one.

BDM

You're deep
like the sea.
Rich in thought
like the treasure that rests beneath,
but most don't know,
or is it that they don't want to?

Skimming the surface has never been a talent of
yours,
and you've lost count
of how many have failed to reach your depths.

Perhaps long-distance and proper technique
aren't strong suits they possess.

But that doesn't mean you stop diving.

I appreciate the fact that you strive for things
that are out of others' capacity.

That just means it will take someone special to
get to you.

I hope they brought a flashlight–
not only to help guide them through your abyss,
but to signal you home.

JDM 4/8/11

I find myself trying not to write about you,
but how am I to help where my mind wanders
off to?
Especially when I hear your voice
echoing through every fiber of my being.

The time I knew you was a time I felt most
alive,
and all I have been doing ever since is trying to
chase that high.

No drug has been able to cut it.
No amount of dopamine will do.
I've traveled from place to place
and still,
nothing has brought me closer to you.

I remember the last conversation we had before
the life left your body.
Your ship once a vessel, now weathered by
suffering
and I could barely recognize it,
but your eyes were still your eyes
and I wasn't ready to say our goodbyes.

You told me how afraid you were of the
unknown
and that brought tears to my eyes.
"How could you possibly think Heaven is real
and you not be a part of it?"
I couldn't think of anyone who would be
deemed more deserving.
Anyone who had the privilege of knowing you
would agree.

I tried not to be selfish,
but I couldn't help but think
that as your agony was ending–
mine was just beginning.
Promised I'd be strong and let you go gracefully,
but I knew differently.
I'd spend the rest of my life trying to find you
again
and mold you into words to keep you alive,
so I could continue to be loved–
in the only way I've ever wanted to be loved– by
you.
And perhaps that is my high.

Kitchen Serenade

The last time I saw you,
I serenaded you in the kitchen
like the good ol days
when things were simple;
we weren't growing older
and you loved my childish ways.

I tried to stop us from becoming
what we always promised we wouldn't,
but you stopped listening
and I refused to not be heard.
Sang songs to soothe,
but even that wouldn't do.

"We aren't kids anymore"
and yet, you can't respond to anything other than
a lullaby.
Kid gloves for everything
because you can't face the reality of what truly
haunts you.

Staying tied. Investment. Follow through.
Not living up to the man you said you'd be,
but a ring, house, or baby won't change what I
already know.

You'll always be the same–
making promises attached to conditions you
can't keep
with the expectation that I'd always stay.
And you'll resent me for living up to my every
word.

We'll soon enough become strangers once more
as if we never knew each other at all,
but the longer I live–the more I understand
that—
I won't ever stop wanting to serenade the one I
love in the kitchen.

Some Trees Don't Bring Peace, Only Shade

The branch I thought was a hand
is now nothing more than a piece of firewood
I'd like to set ablaze.

We no longer burn bright,
but you deserve to be set on fire
for the hell you put me through.

Even on my worst day I never deserved it.

There was no beginning to our friendship,
at least from where I lay my roots;
however, there was an end.

How could I have given
My light, love, and loyalty
to someone who can barely recognize
what it means to be a seed?

The branch has been set so low;
it deserves to be torched.
Maybe then, something tolerable can
rise from the ashes.

Until then, I hope no one mistakes
your plywood for solid oak ever again.

Red Flags

You put me in a dark hole,
a place where I could barely recognize myself.

I made my choices, this is true–
but they were based on words
that turned out to be lies,
so where did the manipulation start?

I reverted back to old ways
due to the sheer anxiety you caused.
Then you had the nerve to judge my vices.
My body was rejecting you
even before I had the chance to.

But how could that be?
When every part of my skin
wants to be felt by your fingers–

I pretend it is your hands that are
skimming my surface;
the one I'm bringing my tide to.
The wave breaks at your shore and we crash.
No one can do it like you.

Perhaps this is the only thing you're good for.

And for a brief moment,
I'm willing to put you in your place,
if you can learn to keep your words to yourself
and only touch me with your hands.

I snap back to reality
and remember you are no longer welcome in this
oasis.
You do not deserve to touch these curves.
You cannot have the lesser half of me–
when I deserve nothing more than
to be cared for in full.

Wandering Washington

Cleansed myself by the creek
after walking miles
through the woods that speak.

I've been set on fire
and much like the leaves
I'm going through a change

Where everything that is green
turn to shades of an interchange:

Yellow, orange, red, and brown–
how they reveal their brightest colors
right before they fall.

As they crumble into dust and die,
they don't regret being what they are
and it never stops them from being reborn again.

But if not a leaf, what else?

I can't stand beneath these branches
and not think about how beautiful it would be
if you were here with me.

But in a strange way, I know that you are;
you're in everything that I do–

in the places I explore,
in the spades I create,
in the conversations that transpire,
in the hearts I inspire.

What has died had rearranged itself
into something else.

I hid amongst the trees,
the only place I could find peace.
I got lost beneath the canopies of color;
managed to find myself there, too.

Love Lost

Why does it seem like time is always fleeting
and I can never catch up to the moments
that I wish I could hold onto forever?

The feeling of being in love–
memorizing the lines in the faces of those we
care for.
The creases in the cheeks
that have made their mark over years of laughter.

A fine line between allowing love in
and not giving it the power to consume me.

I know what can happen when love presents
itself,
the potential it has to shape my entire existence,
or have it come crumbling to pieces–
leaving me in ruins.

How am I supposed to give my heart away,
all the while trying to keep it safe?

It seems as though I can't.
I either have to let it in
with the notion of it destroying me,
or taking me to the place I'm destined to be.

Printed in the USA
CPSIA information can be obtained
at www.ICGtesting.com
LVHW020504101223
766083LV00067B/1792